A WEALTH BUILDERS BLUEPRINT TO BUILD YOUR DREAM INVESTMENT PORTFOLIO

NOWHERE TO GO BUT UP!

"Someone is sitting in the shade today because someone planted a tree a long time ago."

~Warren Buffett

A WEALTH BUILDERS BLUEPRINT TO BUILD YOUR DREAM INVESTMENT PORTFOLIO

NOWHERE TO GO BUT UP!

"Someone is sitting in the shade today because someone planted a tree a long time ago."

~Warren Buffett

NIKHIL GUPTA

Worldwide Publishing by
Pendown Press
Powered by Gullybaba.com

PENDOWN PRESS
Powered by **Gullybaba Publishing House Pvt. Ltd.,**
An ISO 9001 & ISO 14001 Certified Co.,
Regd. Office: 2525/193, 1st Floor, Onkar Nagar-A, Tri Nagar,
Delhi-110035
Ph.: 09350849407, 09312235086
E-mail: info@pendownpress.com
Branch Office: 1A/2A, 20, Hari Sadan, Ansari Road,
Daryaganj, New Delhi–110002
Ph.: 011-45794768
Website: PendownPress.com

First Edition: 2022
Price: ₹299/-

ISBN: 978-93-5554-258-8

Layout and Cover Designed by Pendown Graphics Team
Printed and Bound in India by Thomson Press India Ltd.

Dedication

Dedicated to my family, friends and my team. Without their trust, understanding, support and above all, love, my life is incomplete.

True Love

I would like to especially acknowledge my Guru, Akshar Yadav, for inspiring me to write this book. He is the one who has given perspective to my life and my team. I am always thankful to you, Sir.

Most importantly, my home, my love, my life 'Kaichi Dham', I first met Baba on 11.9.21 and fell in love with him on 11.10.2021. (Jai Neeb Karoli Baba) (Jai Devi Maa) I know you are holding my hand and have brought me home. Whenever I visit you, I feel I have come home.

Please always stand by me.

And above all, my kids, Aayan and Naina.

Contents

Who Should Read This Book?

1. Someone who wants to experience financial freedom in their life.
2. Someone who wants to earn the maximum return in stocks.
3. Someone who wants to grow rich.
4. Someone who wants peace.
5. Someone who is a beginner in the stock market.
6. Someone who is losing money in stocks.

About This Book

Is your money magnifying while you and the stock market are sleeping?

If NOT, you need to STOP EVERYTHING and START READING THIS BOOK. It will show you how to create a Legacy of Stocks. This legacy will help you in earning even while you are sleeping.

The investor is innocent and usually doesn't know the tricks and tips on investing successfully.

Every investor has one goal. They are looking for profits and peace of mind but cannot find a way.

This makes the investor angry and frustrated, leading to health issues such as stress and anxiety due to the financial situations arising in family life and stress transfers in stocks.

They are looking for permanent solutions but are stuck with investing in Fixed Deposits, LIC, Kisan Vikas Patra, etc. These are low-return products and lose money to inflation.

Investors don't understand the real rate of return and the power of return in the stock market.

Investors are keen on fixed deposits, and banks invest the money from fixed deposits into corporate business houses by funding them and making profits. Investors don't understand that they can directly invest in these companies and earn a higher return.

This book teaches you about the fundamentals of stocks and the basic principles of successful investing.It also makes you aware of the basic mistakes people make while investing and shows you how to completely avoid these mistakes.

About The Author

Nikhil Gupta is an alumnus of the prestigious IIM Lucknow and a Law Graduate. He has been working in his Family Legacy Business Pee Aar Securities Limited., a Share Broking firm, since 1995.

He is a member of the Bar Council of Delhi with a Master's in Business Law from NLSIU Bangalore and an MBA (International Business), GGSIPU, AML and CFT Trainer and Researcher in Stocks.

Besides these qualifications, he holds numerous Degrees, Diplomas and Certifications in Business, Audit and Finance.

He holds 18 plus years of experience in the Stock Market, Stock Investing, Financial Planning and Stock Research.

He has trained hundreds of MBA, BBA and BCom students across India and abroad in the Summer Internship Programs.

His areas of interest include Criminal Psychology and Forensic Audit.

Acknowledgements

As a rule, we consider debt as bad, but there is good debt too.

I take pride in carrying a huge 'debt' -albeit a good one, a debt of gratitude – from each of my friends, family, team, staff, and clients, those who personally interacted with me, and those who silently recommended us within their circle of friends and relatives.

I am indebted to YOU.

As much as I would love to name each of you, I am constrained by the available space. I firmly believe that no individual can do anything on their own. Anything worthwhile is born out of feedback, constructive criticism and unwavering faith.

Without all your inputs, this book would not have been feasible. I thank each one of you.

1

Stocks & Market

Understanding SLR and BAP:

- S- Safety
- L- Liquidity
- R- Return

AND

- B- Behavior
- A- Attitude
- P- Psychology

Believe me, the stock, stock market, and financial market revolve around these 6 elements.

Only if you understand these elements will you become a great investor!

TRUST ME, this sounds like LOTS OF ENGLISH, BIT BORING, BUT VERY TRUE and USEFUL, so let's explore them in detail below:

1. Safety

Is Money Safe?: The short answer is yes.

Volatility decreases in the long run. The rags-to-riches stories of many Indian investors highly publicized in the media have become reasons for numerous individuals to be drawn to invest and succeed in the stock markets.

Though awareness of the Indian stock markets is at an all-time high right now, still, not all investors have the knowledge to face and overcome the volatility associated with stock investments and markets. They are not cognizant of the highs and lows of the market.

Many investors have the misguided belief that the stock market is a 'get-rich-quick' method, while some others believe it's a place to make profits when stocks go up, i.e., perform well. That's it.

But there is more to the stock markets than just the stock prices going up and down. Indian stock markets have become quite accessible lately for the common investors, too, and it provides the latter with some amazing advantages and opportunities.

In short, Indian stock markets can help individuals and small investors build wealth.

2. Liquidity

Quick Exit: Today, technology has not only made ordering food online an easy task but even stocks can also be bought and sold **online smoothly** and with ease. Stocks can be bought and sold by investors online with minimum effort; all it takes is a click on their phones.

The moment you opt to buy a stock, the amount for your order is debited from your account. Once the stock reaches the price targeted by you, the stock**s are credited to your account.**

The selling process is similar too. When you opt to sell the stocks, the shares will immediately be debited from your account on reaching the target price. The money from the sale gets credited to your account within 2–3 working days. This new-age ease of buying and selling stocks has made them an immensely liquid investment instrument.

3. Return

Profit: A return is a term basically used from a financial perspective. Simply put, it is the money you make or lose on an investment over a certain period.

A return can also mean the change in the value of the currency of an investment over a certain period.

It is the ratio of profit earned to the original sum of investment. It can also either be the net result on an investment (calculated after deducting any fees, taxes, inflation etc., that may accrue on the investment), or it can be expressed as gross returns meaning only the price change on the investment.

A return is a change in the price of an asset, investment, or project over time, which may be represented in two ways: as price change or expressed in terms of the percentage change.

A positive return is obviously referred to as a profit, and if the return is negative, it is termed a loss.

For ease of calculation and comparison purposes, returns are typically annualized. When a return is calculated for the entire period of holding an investment, it is referred to as a holding period return. It calculates the gain or loss for the entire period and not just annually.

The real return accounts for the effects of inflation and other external factors, while the nominal return is only interested in a price change.

The total return for stocks includes price change as well as dividend and interest payments.

Several return ratios exist for use in fundamental analysis.

4. Behavior

Never say I am always right.

The stock market, like our heart, does not beat or work in a straight line. Like our heartbeat, it rises and falls. However, there is one crucial difference. It is a typical feature of the stock market to rise and fall sharply and steeply.

This sharp rise and fall can largely be attributed to the psyche of the people (read investors) making the financial decisions. In other words, the psychology of its investors drives the stock market. Investors often tend to act irrationally, and this behavior impacts asset prices.

Understanding the behavior of investors can help, therefore, in making strategies that could be used in fetching abnormal returns by exploring systematic errors made by investors while making investment decisions.

Human behavior is nothing but a reaction tothe news;one must understand themself before investing.

The popular financial theory assumes that market participants act rationally to maximize their benefits, and they don't ever make mistakes.

However, behavioral finance challenges the assumptions of the rational actor theory as it applies to markets, investments, and other financial matters.

Behavioral finance draws heavily from cognitive psychology to understand investor behavior in the real world.

5. Attitude

Overconfidence and Social factors.

TV and newspapers news and how we react to this news is an important attitude.

A combination of two critical disciplines, psychology and economics, known as Behavioral Finance, is crucial to understanding the underlying psychology of investors. It helps us understand the investor's psychology that drives their financial decision-making. To understand why and how people make irrational financial decisions when they save, invest, spend, and borrow money.

This involves a delicate mix of personal and social psychology principles with traditional finance theory to explore and understand the stock market performance. Behavioral finance relies on how the human thinking process and errors impact investor choice and prices of the stock exchange.

Please note that as a cardinal rule, investors do not invest rationally as assumed by most investment models, and there exist significant variations in the behavior of investors.

6. Psychology

I am sure you would be shell-shocked if I said that successful investing is not all about number crunching.

Further, you would be even more surprised if I told you that the key player in making critical decisions is your own psychology. The study of the mind and behavior about how people invest can prove to be very useful to investors.

Markets and their moves are often erratic. To invest successfully, we need to be self-aware. We need to be clear whether we are acting based on research, logic and clear thinking or if our instincts are based on emotions. It would be unforgivable if you lost money despite having the right research at your disposal simply because of your irrationality.

One important area that stock-market psychology explores quite a bit is the biases in the thinking of the investors. A bias can be described as a faulty way of thinking that we have become conditioned to.

Here's an example of a bias, The human mind appears to be more sensitive to loss. We have an ingrained instinct of loss aversion. The human mind reacts more intensely to losses than to gains.

Surprisingly we are not as delighted and joyful if we make a profit of 50,000 Rupees, but if we lose 10,000 Rupees, we are devastated. And it is this feeling of devastation that drives investors to panic. Their sensitivity to loss intensifies their panic, leading them to sell the stocks where they incurred the loss and this irrational behavior, when joined by other investors, causes the market to crash.

2

Why Should You Invest At All?

The best way to answer this question would be to show you what the scenario would be if you did not invest at all. Taking a hypothetical example, suppose your earning is Rs. 100,000/- per month, and you spend Rs. 60,000/-towards your expenses such as food, rent, housing, travel & transport, medical, leisure, entertainment etc. The remaining Rs. 40,000/- is the surplus you have every month. To keep this hypothetical calculation simple, we will ignore personal income tax.

Here are the assumptions we have used in our calculations.

- That you get a 10% hike in salary annually.
- That the cost of living inflates by 8% annually.
- That you still have 20 years of earning left. You are now 35 and likely to stop working at 55.
- We are assuming that the expenses will remain fixed.
- And that the surplus of Rs. 40,000/- per month is all in hard cash.

Based on these assumptions, this is what your situation will look like in 20 years.

Years	Annual Income	Annual Expense	Savings
1	12,00,000	7,20,000	4,80,000
2	13,20,000	7,77,600	5,42,400
3	14,52,000	8,39,808	6,12,192
4	15,97,200	9,06,992	6,90,208
5	17,56,920	9,79,552	7,77,368
6	19,32,612	10,57,916	8,74,696
7	21,25,874	11,42,550	9,83,324
8	23,38,460	12,33,954	11,04,508
9	25,72,306	13,32,670	12,39,636
10	28,29,538	14,39,284	13,90,254
11	31,12,490	15,54,426	15,58,064
12	34,23,740	16,78,780	17,44,960
13	37,66,114	18,13,082	19,53,032
14	41,42,726	19,58,130	21,84,596
15	45,56,998	21,14,780	24,42,218
16	50,12,698	22,83,962	27,28,736
17	55,13,968	24,66,678	30,47,288
18	60,65,364	26,64,012	34,01,352
19	66,71,900	28,77,134	37,94,766
20	73,39,090	31,07,304	42,31,786
Total Income	6,87,29,998	3,29,48,614	3,57,81,384

If you analyze these figures, you will know that the situation is dire and worrying.

After 20 years of hard work, what you will have in hand is only Rs. 3.57 Crs.

Since this calculation is based on your expenses being **fixed throughout th**ese 20 years, it means you haven't been able to upgrade your lifestyle at all; all your dreams of a bigger home, a better **car and global** vacation destinations have been suppressed. You have been stagnant all your life.

Also, note that assuming the expenses will continue to grow at 8%, this amount of money can only tide you over 8 years post-retirement. After that, you will literally have no money to live life.

So, **what is the solution to this horrif**ying future? Is there an option to have more money at your disposal to help you live comfortably post-retirement and have a significantly larger sum of money at the end of your 20 years of hard work?

Yes, the solution is Hard Work + Smart Work

Let's consider the option where you don't just keep your surplus as idle cash. Instead, you choose to invest the cash in an option that will grow your money by at least, say, 12% annually.

So if you had a surplus of Rs. 4,80,000/- in the first year and invested it at 12% per annum for 20 years, at the end of 20 years, you would have nearly 24 Cr as compared to just 3.57 Cr without any investment.

Years	Yearly Income	Yearly Expense	Cash Retained	Retained cash Invested @12%
1	12,00,000	7,20,000	4,80,000	41,34,126
2	13,20,000	7,77,600	5,42,400	41,71,038
3	14,52,000	8,39,808	6,12,192	42,03,336
4	15,97,200	9,06,992	6,90,208	42,31,242
5	17,56,920	9,79,552	7,77,368	42,54,974
6	19,32,612	10,57,916	8,74,696	42,74,736
7	21,25,874	11,42,550	9,83,324	42,90,726
8	23,38,460	12,33,954	11,04,508	43,03,132
9	25,72,306	13,32,670	12,39,636	43,12,138
10	28,29,538	14,39,284	13,90,254	43,17,918
11	31,12,490	15,54,426	15,58,064	43,20,636
12	34,23,740	16,78,780	17,44,960	43,20,456
13	37,66,114	18,13,082	19,53,032	43,17,530
14	41,42,726	19,58,130	21,84,596	43,12,006
15	45,56,998	21,14,780	24,42,218	43,04,024
16	50,12,698	22,83,962	27,28,736	42,93,718
17	55,13,968	24,66,678	30,47,288	42,81,222
18	60,65,364	26,64,012	34,01,352	42,66,656
19	66,71,900	28,77,134	37,94,766	42,50,138
20	73,39,090	31,07,304	42,31,786	42,31,786
Total cash after 20 years				853,91,538

So, this example should make it amply clear that your cash balance increases significantly if you invest your surplus/savings. That too at a staggering 2.4x times the regular amount which means that you can live life comfortably worry-free even post-retirement.

So this example makes it clear that there are at least three strong and compelling reasons why you should invest.

1. **To Tackle Inflation:** Inflation is the growing cost of living over the years, which is inevitable. By investing, one can deal better with it.

2. **To Create Wealth:** Investing our money and making it work for us instead of sitting idle can create substantial wealth for us in addition to our regular and fixed sources of income. This can be used to fulfill responsibilities such as education and marriage of children, medical expenditure etc.

3. **To Meet Life's Financial Aspirations:** Investment and its resultant earnings can help us meet our financial aspirations of upgrading our lifestyle. Otherwise, we would stay stagnant and have to suppress all our dreams of a better home, car, gadgets, vacations etc.

3

Where Should You Invest?

So once you understand the reasons behind and the benefits of investing, the next question obviously would be – as to where you should invest and what returns you are likely to receive on that investment.

While deciding where to invest, it is essential that you understand your own risk-taking ability and temperament as also your expectation of return. Then you should choose an asset that suits these qualities and expectations.

An asset can be classified into various classes or categories basis their characteristics of risk and return. Some of the popular asset classes are as below:

1. Fixed income instruments
2. Equity
3. Real estate
4. Commodities (such as Gold & Silver)

Fixed Income Instruments

These are instruments in which one can invest with there being minimal risk to the principal amount invested. A return is paid to the investor in the form of interest on the principal amount basis the type of fixed-income instrument chosen by the investor.

The interest can be paid on a quarterly, half-yearly or annual basis. At the end of the fixed deposit period or the term of deposit known as the maturity period, the entire capital, i.e., the principal, along with interest accrued, is given back to the investor.

Popular fixed income instruments are:

- Fixed deposits offered by banks.
- Bonds issued by the Government of India.
- Bonds issued by Government related agencies such as HUDCO, NHAI, etc.
- Bonds issued by corporate's.
- Since June 2021, the return from a fixed income instrument can vary from 5% and 8%.

Equity

Buying shares of publicly listed companies on the stock exchange is referred to as investing in equity.

These shares are listed and traded on the Bombay Stock Exchange (BSE) and the National Stock Exchange (NSE).

While there exists no capital guarantee on investment in equity, the returns from this category of investment can be highly profitable.

In the last 15 years, the Indian Equities market has had returns of nearly 14% – 15% CAGR (compound annual growth rate).

In some cases, investments into some of the well-run Indian companies have generated even more than 20% CAGR in the long term. Such opportunities for investment take skill, patience, research, and hard work to be identified and leveraged.

If equity investments are held for more than 365 days, and the gains from such investments exceed Rs. 1 lakh, they are liable to be taxed at 10%. This came into effect on 1st April 2018 (previously, such investments were tax-free). Compared to other asset classes, this rate of tax is lower.

Real Estate

Investment in real estate means buying and selling commercial and non-commercial properties. It can mean transacting in plots, sites, Independent homes, apartments and other commercial properties.

Income from real estate investments can be of two types:

- ✓ Capital Gains due to appreciation on the original amount invested
- ✓ Rental income from residential or commercial properties.

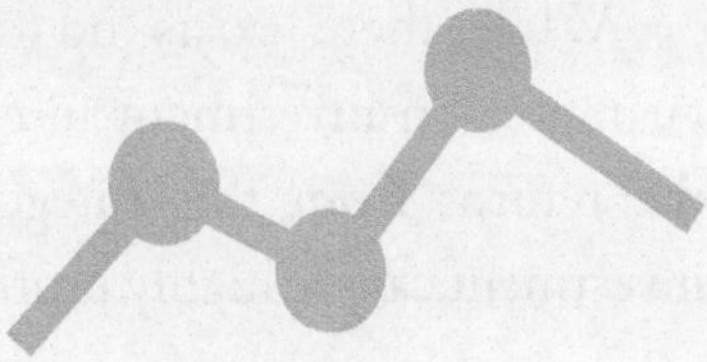

However, the drawback is that real estate transactions can be quite complex with the procedures involving legal verification of documents, registrations, leases, contracts etc. Also, real estate investments are cash-intensive. Also, there is no official metric to measure the returns generated by real estate.

Commodity – Bullion

Investments in gold and silver are considered one of the most popular investment avenues. If we look at the last 20 years or so. Investments in Gold & Silver have shown CAGR returns of nearly 8%. You can invest in Gold & Silver either in the form of jewelry or through Exchange Traded Funds (ETF).

Looking at the average returns from the various forms of investments, it is quite clear that equities are the instruments that tend to offer the best returns, especially over a long period of time.

Power Tips on Investments

As the wise have said from ancient times, putting all your eggs in one basket is inadvisable. Your investments ideally should be a balanced mix of all asset classes. Divide and diversify your investment among the various asset classes to ensure safety as well as significant returns. The technique of allocating money across asset classes is termed 'Asset Allocation.'

Young investors can take higher risks given their age and years of investment available to them. A good thumb rule for young investors to follow should be to allocate around 70% of their investable income into equity, 20% can be invested into precious metals, and it is advisable to invest the rest into fixed income instruments.

As for retired persons, the thumb rule would be to invest about 80% of their savings into fixed income, 10% into equity and the balance 10% into precious metals. The ratio in which an investor allocates their investments across asset classes will depend upon the investor's risk temperament and appetite for returns.

Investing is a great way to enhance your income and live your life fully. However, before investing, you should keep the following in mind...

Risk and return go hand in hand and are inversely proportional. The higher the risk, the higher is likely to be the return and vice-a-versa.

If your aim is to protect your principal amount, it is advisable to invest in fixed income instruments. They are relatively less risky. However, if you take into account the rate of inflation, it is possible you may discover that you have really not got as much return as you thought. Example – A fixed deposit that gives you 5% when the inflation is 6% means you are losing a net 1% per annum. Fixed-income investment is best suited for ultra-risk-averse investors.

Equities are a great instrument of investment. Over a significant period of time, it can beat inflation. Equity investments have generally been seen to generate returns as high as 14-15%. They can be risky, though.

In comparison, Real Estate investment requires a significantly large amount of money and cannot be done at a smaller scale with lesser amounts. Another concern with real estate is liquidity. – Real estate cannot be bought or sold at will. It is always dependent on finding the right time and the right buyer or seller to enter into a transaction with.

Commodity investments such as gold and silver are comparatively safer. However, their return has not been very encouraging.

4

Commonly Used Jargons You Must Know

In this chapter, I will acquaint you with a few of the common market jargon/terminologies and concepts associated with them.

Bull Market (Bullish)

During a particular period, if the stock index keeps rising, the market is referred to as a Bull Market, and when you believe that the stock prices are likely to go up, that means you are bullish on the stock price.

Bear Market (Bearish)

During a particular period, if the stock index keeps falling, the market is referred to as a Bear Market, and when you believe that the stock prices are likely to go down, that means you are bearish on the stock price.

Trend

This is a term that defines the way the market is going, meaning the general direction the market is going toward and how strong that direction is. For example, if the market is declining, the trend is bearish. If it is rising, the trend is bullish. And when there is no movement and the market is flat, then the trend is sideways.

Face Value of a Stock

The fixed denomination of a stock is called its Face value (FV) or par value. Face value plays an important role when any corporate action is involved. Face value comes in handy when dividends and stock splits are announced, or any mergers and acquisitions happen. Dividends are issued keeping the face value in mind. For example, the FV of Infosys is 5, and if they announce an annual dividend of Rs.65/-, then it means the dividend paid is 1300%s (65 divided by 5).

52 Weeks High/Low

A 52 week high is the highest point at which a stock has traded during the last 52 weeks, meaning a year. And the 52 week low is the lowest point at which the stock has traded during the last 52 weeks. These High & Low reference points give an idea of the range of movement between which the stock has traded within that particular year. It is generally believed that when a stock reaches a 52 week high, then it indicates a bullish trend for its near future and vice-versa.

All-Time High/Low

Similar to the 52 weeks high and low, the difference being the all-time high is the highest price the stock has ever traded since it was listed. Likewise, the all-time low price is the lowest price at which the stock has ever traded since being listed.

Upper Circuit/Lower Circuit

The stock exchange places a price band within which the stock can be traded in the market on any given day. The highest point of price the stock can be traded on that day is the upper circuit limit, and the lowest price is the lower circuit limit. These restrictions are put in place by the exchange to protect the stock and investors from excessive volatility in stock as a reaction to any news related to the stock's company.

Long Position

Long Position being Long or having a Long position, or going long is simply a reference to your intent or the direction of your trade. For example, if you buy or have bought or even intend to buy Reliance Industries shares, you are long on Reliance Industries H1 or planning to go long on Reliance Industries, and respectively. Or say if you have bought on the Nifty Index expecting it to trade higher, then you have a long position on Nifty. When you are long on a stock or an index, it means you are bullish on it.

Short Position

Having a Short Position, going short or simply 'shorting' is the description of a transaction that is carried out in a particular order. This concept may be slightly tricky to grasp and understand. To explain shorting better, I'd like to narrate a recent incident that happened to me at work [H2] [H3]

Intraday Position

Intraday Position is a reference to a trading position initiated by you with the aim to square off the position within the very same day.

OHLC

As the acronym suggests, this is very simple to understand. OHLC means Open, High, Low and Close. Open is the price at which the stock opens on any day, high is the highest price at which the stock trades on that day, low is the lowest price at which the stock trades on that same day and close is the closing price of the stock. For example, the OHLC of Reliance Industries Limited on 04.04.2022 was Rs. 2655.45, Rs. 2675, Rs. 2641.65 and Rs. 2663.70 [H5].

Volume

Volumes means the total transactions a stock generated during the day. It includes both buying and selling. These volumes have an impact on the stock prices.

For example, on 04.04.2022, the volume on Reliance Industries Limited was 36,53,737 shares.

Market Segment

A division in which the trade happens for a particular financial instrument is called a market segment. Every financial instrument has its own particular risk and reward parameters. There are three main segments in which the exchange operates.

5

Major Economic Events Impacting The Stock Market

Just buying or selling based only on company-specific information is definitely not enough. Many other events influence the market, and it is vital to have an understanding of these events as well before transacting on the stock market. These events are external factors and may be economic and/or non-economic in nature. However, these events impact the market significantly, so we will explore some of these events with a view to understanding them and also see how the stock market reacts to them.

The Monetary Policy of the RBI

World over, every country has a central governing bank that is responsible for formulating the monetary policy and setting interest rates. In India, this bank is the Reserve Bank Of India (RBI). The RBI controls the supply of money by controlling the interest rates, and the monetary policy is the tool it uses to do this.

The setting of the interest rates ignites a whole chain reaction in the economy; It is a tricky and delicate thing as the RBI has to walk a thin line between growth and inflation, trying to balance both.

To put it simply – if the interest rates are set high, then by default, the borrowing rates will be high too (especially for companies). When corporates find it difficult to borrow, they will be unable to expand and grow; this, in turn, will slow down the economy.

On the flip side, if the interest rates are set low by RBI, borrowing obviously becomes easier. This means companies and consumers both have more money on their hands. In such a scenario, the average spending capacity increases; when sellers sense increased spending capacity, they begin to increase prices to take advantage of the situation, and this is what is known as inflation.

To achieve this balance between growth and inflation, the RBI carefully considers and monitors all the parameters and then arrives at setting key rates. These key rates are critical, and any imbalance in them can result in uncontrollable economic chaos.

The key RBI rates that are essential for you to track and know these:

1. **Repo Rate:** Any bank can borrow money from the RBI when needed. The RBI charges them an interest for it, and this rate of lending by RBI to other banks is known as the repo rate. Obviously, if the repo rate is high, the

cost of borrowing will be high, which means the economy will grow slowly. The current repo rate is 8% in India. Markets don't respond well to repo rates being increased by the RBI.

2. **Reverse Repo Rate:** Reverse Repo Rate, as is clear from the name, is the rate at which RBI borrows money from banks. Banks are always happy to lend RBI money compared to corporates as they are assured that the RBI will not default. However, understand that when RBI borrows money from, and they choose to give it to RBI instead of funding corporates, the supply of money on the banking circuit reduces as a whole. Any increase in the reverse repo rate does not bode well for the economy. It means a tightened supply of money. The current reverse repo rate in India is 7%.

3. **Cash Reserve Ratio (CRR):** As per the RBI, it is mandatory for every bank to maintain some funds with RBI. The amount needed to be maintained is dependent on the CRR. If the CRR increases, it means that more money has been removed from the system, which does not signify well for the economy.

   A meeting of the RBI is held every two months, and then these key rates are reviewed. This is a momentous event that the market carefully waits for and watches. Interest-rate sensitive stocks such as – banks, automobiles, housing finance, real estate, metals, etc. react quickly and sharply to these key rate decisions by the RBI.

Inflation

Inflation can be defined as a sustained increase in the prices of goods and services.

Higher the inflation, the weaker the buying power of currency/money. Let's understand this through an example. Suppose everything remains the same, let's assume every parameter is equal and unchanged, yet the cost of 1 liter of milk goes up from 40 Rs/Ltr to 45 Rs/Ltr; then this increase in price increase is termed as inflation.

Inflation will always occur over a period of time; it is unavoidable, but too high an inflation rate is not healthy for the economy. Markets don't respond well to high rates of inflation. It is a bad signal, a red flag. All Governments work steadfastly towards cutting down the inflation and bringing it to a manageable level.

An Inflation index is generally used to measure inflation. The index going up means inflation is rising and vice-versa.

Inflation indices can be categorized as:

- The Wholesale Price Index (WPI)
- The Consumer Price Index (CPI)

The Wholesale Price Index (WPI) indicates the movement in prices at the wholesale level. It is the price increase/decrease when commodities are sold between organizations, from one organization to another, which is also referred to as B2B selling and not sold to actual consumers.

Inflation can easily be calculated through the WPI. However, it only depicts inflation at the institutional level and does not capture its effect on the consumer.

At the time of writing this, the WPI inflation for March 2022 (predicted) stands at 11.5%-12%.

Consumer Price Index (CPI), on the other hand, depicts the impact of the rise and fall in prices at a retail level. CPI inflation is what really matters to the consumer, the common man. Calculating CPI is quite a detailed process. As CPI isn't a unilateral index. Instead, it is composed of several internal indices. These indices are calculated by classifying consumption patterns into various categories and subcategories in both rural and urban regions.

CPI is one of the critical measures that help in studying the economy. The process of computing CPI takes careful detailing and effort. The CPI Index is published by the Ministry of Statistics and Programme Implementation (MOSPI) in the 2nd week of every month.

The CPI stood at 5.22% in December 2021.

The CPI inflation hit a kind of high at 11.16% in November 2013 and then cooled down for quite some time. However, in the last 2 years, it seems to be on the rise again. As we discussed earlier, the RBI's challenge is to strike a balance between inflation and interest rates. A low-interest rate leads to a rise in inflation, and a high-interest rate tends to arrest inflation.

The Index of Industrial Production (IIP)

The Index of Industrial Production (IIP) is a short-term indicator of how the country's industrial sector is performing and progressing. The Ministry of Statistics and Programme Implementation (MOSPI) releases the data related to this index every month, along with inflation data.

As is clear from the name, it measures the Indian industrial sectors' production against a fixed benchmark, the reference point of 2004-05. At this reference point, the benchmark year is referred to as the base year.

Production data from about 15 different industries is submitted to the ministry. It is then collated by the ministry and released as an index number.

An increasing IIP index is indicative of a growing and healthy industrial environment. The production going up is a positive sign for the economy and markets. On the other hand, a decreasing IIP is indicative of a slow-moving industrial environment and, thus, a negative sign for the markets.

With the changing times, as we become more industrialized as a nation, the importance of the IIP has gone up. Simply put, an upward graph in industrial production augurs well for the economy, and a downward graph signals an alarm, a wake-up call.

A lower IIP presents a challenge for the RBI to lower interest rates and yet prevent inflation.

The graph shows the change in IIP in percentage terms for the last 5 years.

Purchasing Managers Index (PMI)

The Purchasing managers' index (PMI) is an economic indicator that tries to capture, collate and present business activity occurring across the country's manufacturing and service sectors.

This index is based on a survey where the respondents, specifically the purchasing managers, indicate their change in business perception for the previous month.

For the service and manufacturing sectors, a separate survey is conducted. Then the data from the survey are consolidated on a single index. The survey is conducted with reference to output, business expectations, new orders, and the employment scenario.

The PMI number usually oscillates around 50. A figure upwards of 50 is indicative of expansion, and a figure below 50 is indicative of a contraction or slowdown in the economy. A reading of 50 indicates the status quo, meaning the economy is stagnant.

Budget

A Budget is perhaps the most important and eventful economic event of the year. During this event, the Ministry of Finance discusses the country's finance and financial allotments in a detailed manner. On behalf of the ministry, the Finance Minister makes a budget presentation to the entire country in the parliament.

The budget is of vital importance in the economy as major policy announcements and economic reforms across various sectors are unveiled, and they impact various industries and services greatly.

Now let me show you by illustration how such external events as the budget can affect the stock market directly.

Before the budget of February 2021, there was great anticipation that duties on cigarettes were likely to be increased. The government didn't disappoint. True to expectations; the Finance Minister raised the duties on cigarettes. This led to a hike in cigarette prices.

And these were the implications:

1. There is a likelihood of smokers feeling discouraged from buying cigarettes due to the increased prices (this, of course, is subject to debate). Reduced sales impact the profitability of the cigarette manufacturing companies such as ITC etc. And when profitability decreases, there is a chance that investors may be prompted to sell their ITC stock.

2. When more investors start selling ITC stocks, then the markets will show a downward trend as ITC is an index heavyweight.

Unsurprisingly as a reaction to the budget announcement, ITC traded 3.5% lower.

As is common knowledge, the budget is presented annually, usually in the last week of February.

However, there is the provision that under certain special circumstances, such as a new government formation or any other emergency situation, the budget announcement can be delayed.

Corporate Earnings Announcement

This can be said to be the event to which the stocks react most sensitively.

All the companies listed and trading on the stock exchange are mandated to publicly declare their earnings figures once every quarter. These figures are referred to as the "Quarterly Earnings Numbers". These announcements include details on various operational activities such as:

1. The revenue generated by the company.
2. How has the company managed its expenses?
3. What amount of money did the company pay as taxes and interest charges?
4. What has been the profitability during the quarter?

Some companies also choose to give a preview of their expectations in the upcoming quarters. This forecast is called 'corporate guidance'.

Till now, every quarter, the first blue-chip company to make the quarterly announcement has been Infosys Limited.

They also regularly give guidance. Most market participants keenly follow Infosys for guidance as it tends to impact the markets on an overall basis.

The table below gives you an overview of the earning season in India:

S.No.	Months	Quarter	Result Announcement
01	April to June	Quarter 1 (Q1)	1st week of July
02	July to September	Quarter 2 (Q2)	1st week of October
03	October to December	Quarter 3 (Q3)	1st Week of Jan
04	January to March	Quarter 4 (Q4)	1st Week of April

When a company declares its earnings on a quarterly basis, the investors match the earnings declared with their own expectations of what they expected the company to earn. This form of expectation is referred to as 'street expectation'.

If the company's earnings exceed the 'street expectation', the stock price will react positively. While the stock price will react negatively if the declared earnings do not match up to the 'street expectation.'

If the street expectation and actual numbers match, then the stock price tends to trade flat with a negative bias more often than not, as the company could not pull off any positive surprises.

6

Common Investor And Trader Blunders & How To Avoid Them!

Friends, here I am sharing with you below an almost exhaustive list of the common fatal mistakes that investors make. Later in the chapter, we will discuss them in detail one by one.

- No Trading Plan
- Chasing After Performance
- Not Regaining Balance
- Ignoring Risk Aversion
- Forgetting Your Time Horizon
- Not Using Stop-Loss Orders
- Letting Losses Grow
- Averaging Down or Up
- The Importance of Accepting Losses
- Believing False Buy Signals

- Buying With Too Much Margin
- Running With Leverage
- Following the Herd
- Keeping All Your Eggs in One Basket
- Shirking Your Homework
- Buying Unfounded Tips
- Watching Too Much Financial TV
- Not Seeing the Big Picture
- Trading Multiple Markets
- Forgetting About IT
- The Danger of Overconfidence
- Inexperienced Day Trading
- Underestimating Your Abilities
- The Bottom Line
- Not Understanding the Investment
- Falling in Love with a Company
- Too Much Investment Turnover
- Attempting to Time the Market
- Waiting to Get Even
- Failing to Diversify
- Letting Your Emotions Rule

Having No Concrete Trading Plan in Place

It is best to get into stock trading with at least a basic, if not an extremely well-defined, plan in place. After researching, you should work out your entry and exit points, i.e., you must decide on the amount of capital you'd like to invest, and also have at least a ballpark idea of the maximum loss that you are willing to bear.

However, beginners often make the mistake of not having any trading plan before they begin. Even if they do have a plan, they are often prone to stray from the defined plan as opposed to experienced investors. Novice traders may make the mistake of reversing course altogether out of the blue. For example, they may go short after initially buying securities because the share price is declining — and may end up getting whipsawed.

Chasing after Performance

Another huge mistake people make is focusing on, following and investing in asset classes, strategies, managers, and funds based that are currently performing strongly. They suffer from FOMO (the fear of missing out). They feel they will miss out on great returns if they do not do so. Believe me, this FOMO on great returns has probably resulted in more bad investment decisions than all other factors put together.

However, they forget that If a certain asset class, strategy, or fund has been performing consistently well for some time, it could be nearing or reaching the end of the cycle of its great performance. It could be that the smart money is beginning to move out, and the dumb money is beginning to pour in.

Not Regaining Balance

Rebalancing is a tricky but necessary process that pays well in the long run. It means returning your portfolio to its target asset allocation as originally decided in your investment plan. You may find it challenging because it can sometimes mean selling the asset class that is currently performing well for you and investing more in your worst-performing asset class.

This contrarian and paradoxical action proves especially difficult for newbie investors.

However, it is crucial to rebalance your portfolio as a portfolio that drifts with market returns means that asset classes will be overweight at market peaks and underweighted at market lows — and this is a surefire formula for poor performance. No matter how challenging, you must rebalance your portfolio religiously if you wish to reap the rewards in the long term.

Ignoring Risk Aversion

Understanding your risk temperament and level of risk tolerance is vital to success. However, often investors tend to overlook this and do not invest according to their risk-taking capability.

Low-risk tolerance investors who can't stomach volatility and the ups and downs associated with the stock market or more speculative trades would do well to invest in the blue-chip stocks of established firms as opposed to more volatile shares of start-up companies.

Remember that return on investment always comes with a risk. The lowest risk investment available in India is bills, bonds, and notes. From there, as you move up the risk ladder, various types of investments will offer larger returns to compensate for the higher risk. But never lose sight of the risk involved.

If an investment looks extremely attractive in terms of returns, also review its risk profile carefully and figure out how much money you stand to lose if things go wrong.

DO NOT invest more than you can afford to lose.

Forgetting Your Time Horizon

While investing, always keep a time horizon in mind. Doing so can prove harmful and frustrating. First, think carefully that the funds you are investing will not be needed by you during the period you are investing them for. Only invest what is surplus. Also, work out how long [the time horizon] — you need to save up for your retirement, a down payment on a home, a car, college education or wedding expenditure for your child.

For example,If planning funds to buy a house, it should be a medium-term investment horizon. However, if the aim is to build funds for a child's future college education, it would be more of a long-term horizon investment. Finally, If you are saving for your retirement, say 25–30 years down the line, in that case, you really don't need to be alarmed about how the stock market behaves this year or the next couple of years.

Once you figure out your horizon, you can go ahead and find investments that match that profile.

Not Setting Up Stop-Loss Orders

If you don't have a trading plan in place, it automatically follows that you have not set up stop-loss orders to minimize your losses. These can be of many varieties and can limit your losses due to any adverse movement in either a stock or the entire market.

All you have to do is set up the parameters, and the orders will get executed automatically once the parameters are met.

Setting up tight parameters means that losses will be capped before they become sizeable. But there is a flip side risk too. A stop order on long positions may be implemented at levels below those specified should the security suddenly gap lower — as happened to many investors during the Flash Crash.

However, even keeping that in mind, the benefits of stop-orders outweigh the risk of stopping out at an unplanned price.

Letting Losses Grow

Not moving on quickly to the next trade idea after they sustain a small loss on some asset is another critical mistake that investors make. They become stuck on it even when a trade goes against them. They keep hoping that, eventually, things will work out, and thus, their losses keep mounting.

On the other hand, successful traders move on quickly to the next idea.

Averaging Down or Up

If you are trading in the blue-chip stock, it is great to average down on a long position if your investment horizon is long.

However, the same will not apply to a person who is trading in volatile or riskier assets. If a trader makes the mistake of keeping on adding to a losing position, the losses will become very damaging and unmanageable. The entire position will need to be given up.

Another common mistake made by novice traders is that they tend to average up and go short rather than conservative investors because they feel security is advancing rather than declining. This is also a very risky move.

Accepting Losses

Investors are just normal people, and people have their own human shortcomings and flawed judgements. Even the greatest and sharpest of investors can make mistakes. However, often investors fail to accept this simple fact.

Don't keep fretting about a bad investment; say, for example, you made an impulsive stock purchase or one of your star earners suddenly nosedives; the best way would be to just take it in your stride and move on to the next decision of either waiting or watching or maybe getting rid of it.

Play it cool; don't let your pride and ego take center stage. Think of your bank account. Don't keep holding on to a losing investment out of pride or keep buying more shares of the stock now that it is cheaper.

Don't just buy because the price has dropped. It may not necessarily be a good buy. Try to research and analyze the reason behind that drop and price before jumping in.

Believing False Buy Signals

Do not treat stocks as commodities, don't follow the bargain basement tactics with them. Do not just indiscriminately buy stocks because they are selling cheaply. More often than not, there is a strong fundamental reason for a price decline. Research thoroughly and analyze a stock's outlook before you invest in it. The very reasons the stocks are trading low, such as a CEO's resignation, Internal fighting, increased competition etc., could also be the reason that the stock might not increase in value later.

The aim should always be to invest in companies that are likely to experience sustained growth in the future.

Buying With Too Much Margin

Margin means purchasing securities using borrowed money from your broker. These are usually futures and options.

Delving in margins can be beneficial in making money quickly, but it can also result in exaggerated losses.

Get a clear understanding of margins and how they work. Do not make the mistake of treating it as free money.

If you use margin and your investment doesn't go the way you planned, then you end up with a large pile of debt obligations for nothing. Using margin is like buying stocks with your credit card; would you ever do that?

If you are using margin, you will need to monitor your positions very closely, so ensure you have that bandwidth of time before you jump in. Even small movements in price can lead to exaggerated gains and losses that can be disastrous.

Handling Leverage

Leverage, as the cliché in investment circles, goes is not to be taken lightly. It is a double-edged sword that should be yielded carefully because when trades are going profitably, it can boost returns, but at the same time, it can also enhance the losses on losing trades.

So, here's a warning: Do Not Rush Into Using Leverage!

Beginner traders often fall prey to the dazzling degree of leverage they possess — more so in forex (FX) trading. — However, they will soon find out that excessive leverage can destroy trading capital in a flash. Take an example: If there is a leverage ratio of 50:1, which is quite common in retail forex trading — even a 2% adverse move can wipe out an investor's trading capital.

Following the Herd

New traders follow the herd blindly; due to this, at times, either they end up paying too much for hot stocks or take short positions in securities that have already plunged as much as they would and are actually on the cusp of turning around.

Experienced traders know when to exit a trade at the right time. When things start getting too crowded, and the dumb money starts to pour in; they make a quick exit. New traders often do not know when to make an exit. They keep staying in a crowded trade because they lack the courage to go contrary when needed.

Keeping All Your Eggs in One Basket

Diversification is the key to being successful. Do not overexpose yourself to any one investment. Keeping your portfolio versatile with a mix of multiple investments will balance things out and protect you if any of your investment loses money. This will help maintain equilibrium in your portfolio and safeguard you against volatility and extreme price movements in any one investment. And, if one asset class in your portfolio is underperforming, another asset class can balance it out because it may be performing better.

Many studies have proved that most managers and mutual funds underperform their benchmarks. Over the long term, low-cost index funds are typically upper second-quartile performers or better than 65%-to-75% of actively managed funds. Despite all of the evidence in favor of indexing, the desire to invest with active managers remains strong.

It is advisable to index all or at least a substantial portion, say 70%-to-80% of your traditional asset classes. However, I understand that it is difficult to resist the exciting urge to pursue and invest in the next great performer, so here's a hack; set aside around 20%-to-30% of each asset class to allocate to active managers. This will fulfill your desire to pursue outperformance while keeping your portfolio intact.

Shirking Your Homework

Trading is such a volatile and sensitive process, it requires detailed research, due diligence and a lot of homework. However, new traders make the mistake of shirking their homework before entering a trade.

Beginners often are not well versed with the timings of critical data release, trading patterns or seasonal trends. Therefore it is critical for them to do their homework diligently if they want their investments to pay off. They sometimes get overwhelmed by the fear of missing out and are driven by the urgency to make a trade without due diligence leading to losses and an expensive lesson.

Research is helpful in understanding what you are getting into. If you plan to invest in a stock, then you must research the company and its business plans.

It is indeed possible to identify great investments by doing great research.

Buying Basis Unfounded Tips

It wouldn't be wrong to say that at some point or the other, probably every investor makes this mistake in their career.

You might overhear friends or family talking about a stock that, according to their sources, will be bought out, give killer earnings or is about to release a unique path-breaking product.

All these things could be true, of course. However, that does not necessarily mean that the stock being referred to is "God's Gift to Mankind" or "The Next Big Thing".

Don't just rush into your online brokerage account to place a buy order based on these unfounded, unverified tips.

Beware of another major source of such unfounded tips. The culprits here are the investment professionals on television and social media who often tout and hype up a certain stock as though it's a must-buy and it would be criminal not to buy it immediately. In reality, though, this particular product may be nothing more exciting than the flavor of the day.

Keep in mind that buying based on media hype is nothing but a speculative gamble.

This, of course, doesn't mean that you should not pay heed to any stock tips at all. But before you actually act on a tip, you must first consider and verify the source. The next step, as we discussed above, is to do your own due diligence so that you go into the trade with your eyes wide open.

So your buying should be based on whether the investment is right for you, and not just because a fancy mutual fund manager said so in a media interview.

So basically, before acting on a hot tip, play it cool, calmly do some research, do a background check on the company, and seek a second opinion from other investors or unbiased financial advisors if you feel the need to.

Overdosing on Financial TV

This one is actually a no-brainer; there is actually nothing on financial news shows that can help you crack the stock-trade code.

Think of it like this, if anyone really had stock tips for profitable trades, useful trading advice, or had devised a secret formula to make huge killings in the stock market, would they really just broadcast it on TV for all and sundry to use. Or talking of newsletters; would they really sell it to you for a paltry Rs.2,000 per month?

Yes! You know the answer; I already told you it's a no-brainer. They'd shut up and make their millions and would definitely not need to sell a newsletter to make a living, right?

So take financial advice from TV and newsletters with a pinch of salt and due diligence.

Not Seeing the Big Picture

For a long-term investor, one of the most important but often overlooked things to do is a qualitative analysis, which in simple terms means looking at the bigger picture. The brand name in itself also is a very valuable indicator. Take coke, for example; it's a hugely well-known brand. The financial value of the name alone is measured in billions of dollars.

But life can sometimes throw a wrench in the wheels.

So, just financial statements and billion-dollar values alone cannot guarantee success.

Look around you at the big picture, and see what is next on the horizon; technically, in the 1980s, a typewriter company doing well could have been a good investment, but with the advent of personal computers....typewriter companies became a dead investment.

The same was the scenario with Kodak cameras and reels and the advent of digital photography and mobile devices.

So don't ever forget to assess a company from a qualitative standpoint. It is as important as looking at its sales and earnings. It is one of the most potent tools for judging a potential investment.

Trading Multiple Markets

Beginners often tend to flit from market to market — that is, from stocks to options to currencies to commodity futures, and so on. While having a mixed portfolio is advisable, trading multiple markets without the necessary experience right in the beginning can be a huge distraction for the novice trader and may prevent them from gaining the experience necessary to excel in one market.

Forgetting About IT

In your excitement about earning big on the stock market, don't forget the income tax consequences. Most of your earnings will be taxable. Though some investments, such as municipal bonds, will offer you tax breaks before you invest, try to work out what your actual return will be after adjusting for tax, taking into account the investment, your tax bracket, and your investment time horizon.

Also, be careful about the brokerage you pay. Shop around to find a reasonably good broker who doesn't charge you a bomb. Do not pay more than you need to on trading and brokerage fees. Also, don't trade too frequently. Hold on to your investment as much as profitably possible; this will save you money on brokerage.

The Danger of Overconfidence

Trading, as I've shared earlier, is not a get-rich-quick scheme. It is a very demanding occupation. Often when investors start out, they experience "beginner's luck" this sometimes leads them to believe that trading is a shortcut to quick & easy wealth.

Such overconfidence is dangerous as it encourages excessive risk-taking.

Inexperienced Day Trading

Day trading can be a dangerous game and should be attempted only by the most seasoned investors. It is not just enough to be investment savvy. To be a successful day trader, one needs an extra advantage, and for that, they may even need special equipment that is not easily available to the average trader.

Also, before you jump into it, keep in mind that being a day trader can be a significant expense. An average day-trading workstation, along with the software, can cost around tens of thousands of dollars?

Also, you will require a significant amount of trading capital to be able to maintain an efficient day-trading strategy.

Speed is of great consequence in the efficiency of day-trading. Online brokers' systems are not quite fast enough to service the true day trader; literally, pennies per share can make the difference between a profitable and losing trade.

It is highly recommended that investors who wish to be day-traders should take day-trading courses before getting started.

Do Not Take Day Trading Lightly!

Unless you have the expertise, a platform, and access to speedy order execution, do not venture into it.

Underestimating Your Abilities

The stock market is no one's monopoly. With the right learning, skills, tips, techniques and hard work, you can excel at it just as anyone else can.

Some investors tend to believe that they can never excel at investing because stock market success is reserved for sophisticated investors only.

This perception has no truth at all.

Do Not Underestimate Yourself!

With a little time devoted to learning and research, investors can become well-equipped to control their own portfolios and investing decisions, all while being profitable. Remember, much of investing is sticking to common sense and rationality.

Besides having the potential to become sufficiently skilful, individual investors do not face the liquidity challenges and overhead costs of large institutional investors. Any small investor with a sound investment strategy has just as good a chance of beating the market, if not better than the so-called investment gurus. Don't assume that you are unable to successfully participate in the financial markets simply because you have a day job.

Not Understanding the Investment

As an investor, one of the biggest mistakes you can make is investing in a company whose business model you do not understand. This piece of advice has come from one of the world's most successful investors, Warren Buffet. This is because you will be unable to make informed decisions about your investment because you do not fully understand their concept and working

A great way to avoid this is to build a diversified portfolio of Exchange Traded Funds (ETFs) or mutual funds. If you do invest in individual stocks, make sure you thoroughly understand each company those stocks represent before you invest.

Falling in Love with a Company

When a company we've invested in does well, we tend to fall in love with it and love, as the saying goes, is blind. Blindfolded by this love, we forget that we bought the stock as an investment; we forget to keep things practical and professional and make them personal.

Remember, you bought this stock to make money. Life in You never promised to stick to it for life through thick and thin. If any of the fundamentals that prompted you to buy into the company change, consider divorcing the relationship and selling the stock without any guilt or second thoughts.

Lack of Patience

A slow and steady approach to portfolio growth will yield greater returns in the long run. Expecting a portfolio to do something other than what it is designed to do is a recipe for disaster. This means you need to keep your expectations realistic with regard to the timeline for portfolio growth and returns.

Too Much Turnover in Investments

Turnover, or jumping in and out of positions, is another return killer. Unless you're an institutional investor with the benefit of low commission rates, the transaction costs can eat you alive — not to mention the short-term tax rates and the opportunity cost of missing out on the long-term gains of other sensible investments.

Attempting to Time the Market

Trying to time the market also kills returns. Successfully timing the market is extremely difficult. Even institutional investors often fail to do it successfully. A well-known study, "Determinants of Portfolio Performance " (Financial Analysts Journal, 1986), conducted by Gary P. Brinson, L. Randolph Hood, and Gilbert L. Beebower, covered American pension fund returns. This study showed that, on average, nearly 94% of the variation of returns over time was explained by the investment policy decision. 2 In layperson's terms, this means that most of a portfolio's return can be explained by the asset allocation decisions you make, not by timing or even security selection.

Waiting to Get Even

Getting even is just another way to ensure you lose any profit you might have accumulated. It means that you are waiting to sell a loser until it gets back to its original cost basis. Behavioral finance calls this a "cognitive error." By failing to realize a loss, investors are actually losing in two ways. First, they avoid selling a loser, which may continue to slide until it's worthless. Second, there's the opportunity cost of the better use of those investment dollars.

Not Diversifying Enough

While professional investors may be able to generate alpha (or excess return over a benchmark) by investing in a few concentrated positions, common investors should not try this. It is wiser to stick to the principle of diversification. In building an Exchange Traded Fund (ETF) or mutual fund portfolio, it's important to allocate exposure to all major spaces. In building an individual stock portfolio, include all major sectors. As a general rule of thumb, do not allocate more than 5% to 10% to any one investment.

Don't Let Your Emotions Rule

Perhaps the No.1 killer of investment return is impulse and emotion.

The axiom that fears and greed rule the market is true.

Investors should not let fear or greed control their decisions. Don't let your emotions get the better of you; instead, focus on the bigger picture. Stock market returns may deviate wildly over a shorter time frame, but, over the long term, historical returns for large-cap stocks can average 15%.

Over a long time horizon, a portfolio's returns should not deviate much from those averages. In fact, patient investors may benefit from the irrational decisions of other investors.

7

The Bottom Line

Now that I have shared with you in detail the psyche, anatomy, behavior, tips, the pitfalls and how to avoid them with you in detail, you are now equipped to begin your investor journey to building a profitable portfolio.

If you have the money to invest and follow the guidance in this book to avoid the pitfalls that most beginners get trapped in and do your research diligently, you could make your investments pay off smoothly and effortlessly, taking you closer to your financial goals.

These could be anything from marriage, to self-education, to your children's education, your retirement lifestyle fund, the dream home(s), vacations etc.

As reiterated earlier, the stock market can be volatile and sensitive, and with its penchant for producing large gains (and losses), there is no shortage of faulty advice and irrational decision making.

As an individual investor, my advice to you is simple: The best thing you can do to pad your portfolio for the long term is to implement a Rational Investment Strategy that you are comfortable with and willing to stick to.

If you are looking to make a big win by betting your money on your gut feelings, try a casino or buy lotto tickets. The stock market is no joke. Follow the advice shared in this book from my years of learning and experience, take pride in your investment decisions, and in the long run, your portfolio will grow to reflect the soundness of your actions.

Your Stock Broker Could Be Taking You For A Ride And Goading You Into Taking Investment Decisions That Benefit Him.

Case Study 1

One of my high net worth clients (name not disclosed for privacy reasons) who used to invest with two leading broking houses (again, names can't be disclosed) was not comfortable with the false promises made by the investment advisors of the other broking houses.

He approached me through a common friend to get some idea on investments or the suggestions we give to our clients.

Because of his earlier experiences, he was a hard nut to crack.

After several meetings and on-call discussions, we finalized two stocks, to begin with.

First was Fine organic (year 2019), bought on an average of Rs. 1650, quantum invested Rs. 50 lakhs, sold after 3 months at Rs. 2400. Today as of 17.5.2022, the current market price is Rs 4229.

The second stock I recall we finalized was ITC, bought in 2022 February at a price Rs. 202, quantum amounting Rs. 70 lakhs, not sold to date, and the current market price is Rs. 278.

And many more stocks to quote.

In the past three years of our relationship with this client, my major suggestions were Reliance Industries, HDFC Bank, ITC, Infosys, GAIL, TCS, Wipro etc.

He is the one who brought Fine Organic to my notice. I studied the financials of the company and made my suggestions.

Case Study 2

In Covid times, poor people are buying toilet paper, and rich people are buying Stocks.

This is an irony of life that in tough times you balance your mind and your portfolio.

Is everything on fire, or a ray of hope can be seen behind the bushes?

Here is another case of my super-duper high net worth corporate.

They have been my client since 2015 and always bought tax-free government securities from me.

Equity broking, he was doing with a leading discount broker.

Due to service issues, he wanted to shift the equity broking and investment services, however.

After a few negotiations (as we are expensive brokers and a full-fledged broking house), he was okay with making investments through us.

Before 2020, the debt portfolio was amounting Rs. 10 Crore.

We finalized the deal in Covid times, just after the lockdown in March 2020. My office was closed, and all staff was working from home, I was the only one handling servers and other back-office stuff, as I was the only one in the office who got an e-pass from the Delhi government.

He bought Infosys at Rs. 450 in March 2020, Reliance Industries at Rs. 998, TCS at Rs. 1665, ITC at Rs. 175 and many more stocks that I cannot recall, as on day to day 17.5.2022, all stocks are 3 times the price or 4 times the price plus dividend plus bonus, and many more freebies.

With the help of knowledge and information, timely decisions and above all, blessings from the sky, we can earn in the stock market. Good equity makes a good portfolio and gives us a good return on investment, leading to financial freedom.

Case Study 3

One of our clients (an NRI) was approached by a leading investment house in the USA to make a PMS investment with them. The client invested Rs. 400 crores with them, and the yearly fees were Rs. 20 crores to manage the portfolio.

After one year, Rs. 100 crores were wiped off. Yet the broking house sent the bill of Rs. 20 crores to manage the portfolio effectively.

You see how difficult the fund management service can be. An advisor or a broker can take you for a ride, make false promises and burn your hard-earned tax paid money.

With us, In India, he just wants to diversify the portfolio and didn't want much exposure in India.

Still, we managed to crack a deal worth Rs. 4 crores in Mutual Funds and Rs. 6 crores in Direct Equity.

In a span of 2 years in Mutual Fund, the invested capital became Rs. 7 crores and redemption is done.

Equity grew from 6 crores to Rs. 10 crores in a span of 3 years, and money got remitted from India with good profit.

My Gift For You

Since you are serious about investing wisely and building a profitable and safe portfolio, I have a gift for you.

Combined with the learnings from this book, this gift will lead you to the path of effortless prosperity, and you will have nowhere to go but Up, Up and Up!

So here's the fabulous gift!!!!

My portfolio advising service normally costs Rs. 4999 plus GST for 2 hours.

To the readers of this book, this service is free of cost.

Please connect with my team at nikhil@Peeaarmail.com to avail free portfolio advising service.

